from FATHERLESS *to* DADDY'S GIRL

Carmella D. Chandler

Copyright © 2019, Carmella D. Chandler
Contact the Author via e-mail at
authorcarmellachandler@gmail.com.
All rights reserved. No part of this book may be reproduced, stored in a retrieved system, or transmitted in any form or any means, electronic, mechanical, photocopying, recording, scanning, or otherwise, without the prior written permission of the author.

Author: Carmella D. Chandler
Publication Services–Kingdom News Publication Services, LLC.

DISCLAIMER
All the material contained in this book is provided for educational and informational purposes only. No responsibility can be taken for any results or outcomes resulting from the use of this material.
While every attempt has been made to provide information that is both accurate and effective, the author does not assume any responsibility for the accuracy or use/misuse of this information.

Printed in the United States of America.
ISBN 978-0998026244

U.S. Copyright Office
101 Independence Ave. S.E.,
Washington, D.C. 20559-6000

All rights reserved.

KINGDOM NEWS TODAY
Publication Services, LLC

Dedication

I would like to dedicate this book to my mother, Lena Chandler. Thank you for imparting your strong Christian values in my life. Thank you for your support and love throughout my life.

I would also like to dedicate this book to my father, Carl Chandler. Now that I am older, I truly understand the complexity of relationships. So, I pray that this would not be difficult for you, but I am thankful that we have a restored relationship and that we continue to walk in forgiveness.

This story had to be told not to bring shame to me or my family, but to help others. My past of insecurities has been washed away and now I am a very confident woman who understands that the pain from my past has purpose and why I had to experience these things.

I love my family – my mother, my father, my siblings, and my children.

Introduction

"When my father and my mother forsake me, then the Lord will take me up."
Psalms 27:10 KJV

I am so excited about this book! Finally, my prayer has been answered because you have this treasure in your hand. This is not just another book; it is about the message I had received from God as I journeyed through the turbulent sea of "fatherlessness." This book is a fruit of my obedience to God.

I am writing under the inspiration and anointing of the Holy Spirit to every young girl, lady, wife, and mother who has been painfully deprived of the love, warmth, care, presence, assurance and comfort of a good father. I want you to know that there is wholeness and love in God, our Heavenly Father, who is not distant from the trials and challenges that you may be going through right now.

Fortunately, I am a living testimony. For most of my life, I grew up without my earthly father. It was a painful experience which almost marred my entire life. However, today, I am grateful to God for the wonderful lessons I learned from my experience. I am grateful because the love of my Heavenly Father came in to fill the void and heal the heartache that I struggled with for most of my "fatherless life."

This book contains my personal story and insights that will let you in on the reality of the pain of "fatherlessness" and the possibility of finding rest and wholeness in God our Heavenly Father. He never fails, He will not leave or abandon His children, no matter what!

The good news is, we didn't just evolve, we are not an outcome of a random occurrence or evolutionary accident. We were created by God. He is our source and our Father.

God created heaven and earth to be a reflection of His divine nature and the practical expression of His eternal purpose. The bible says, God created the earth out of nothing; yet, there is another distinct and significant perspective to this truth. The bible teaches in Hebrews 1:3 that, God created and holds the entire universe together by the word of His power.

We understand through the Gospel that Jesus is the word of God and He is one and the same with God the Father. Therefore, in John 1:1-3, we can safely infer that God created the heaven and earth from Himself.

God is the source of heaven and earth, the living and non-living things. God is the source of everything and more importantly, the source of everyone. We see in Genesis 1:26

where, God created man in His own image and after His own likeness.

> "...Adam was the son of God."
> Luke 3:38 NLT

This implies, that God is the source of every human, starting from Adam who had no natural father. He was created by God, His Father and the Father of all creation. The truth is, we have our ancestry in God. When Adam lived in the Garden of Eden, he did not live like an orphan; rather, he lived in the full consciousness of a loving and caring father.

Thankfully, God has not reserved this experience for Adam and Eve alone; He has benevolently extended fatherly love and family relationship to each and every one of us.

Who is a Father?

According to the Hebrew meaning of the word "father," it is more than just the head or founder of a household or family; a father is a "source." The good news is that, regardless of the pain, deprivation and suffering that we have had to endure because of our detachment from our physical "source," we can be restored with the hope of connecting to the stable, secure and eternal source of love and provision through God, our Heavenly Father.

A Father is Protector

Have you ever felt insecure, fearful and vulnerable? If yes, then when it comes to shielding a child from harm, hurt or attack, the role of the father cannot be overemphasized. Adam was always confident in the protection and safety that God, His Father provided in the Garden of Eden.

Naturally, every child looks up to their father for protection against bullies, conflicts, commotions, riots and any other attack. A daughter always rests in the ability of her father to protect her.

A Father is the Source of Manifold Provision

Abundance and lack always leave their imprint on the clay of our human existence. When children are deprived of physical, emotional and spiritual nourishment, the daunting signs of a weak body, feeble mind and crushed spirit are inevitable.

Understandably, children need nourishment, good shelter and many other things that can only be abundantly available through the provision of a good "Daddy."

Likewise, it is possible to have Daddy physically present but emotionally, financially and morally absent from the home and distant from the lives of his children. Love is a gift that must be expressed through giving.

Certainly, the pain of separation from a loving father can be so enormous, there is no better counselor and guide than a loving father. God has reserved a place in the heart of every child that longs for the advice, correction and direction from a good father.

When a Daughter Longs for the Comfort of Daddy's Embrace in Times of Despair

The comfort and kind words of a father can lift any burden. There is a sense of assurance and hope that comes from the father to a child who has been heart broken by life's situation. This often results to emotional wounds that may fester for many years.

"Fatherless"

On the other hand, what does it mean to be called "Fatherless?" Here are some definitions I was able to come up with:

- It means not having a father living, or lacking a father's protection.
- Not knowing the identity of one's father.
- An unused root meaning of being lonely, bereaved or an orphan.

You might have lost your self-esteem, morality, dignity, opportunity and pride because of "Daddy issue" nevertheless, I want you to know that there is hope and restoration in God!

This book is for every young girl or woman, who has ever experienced daddy issues. Whether abandoned, rejected, deceased or just never knew him. You do not have to feel unloved or not good enough.

As you read this life changing book, I pray that you will find the strength to finally move past bitterness, brokenness, despair, rejection and hurt to forgiveness, wholeness, hope, acceptance and healing. You are a lovely princess and an adorable queen!

Even more, I release upon you the spirit of understanding, that equips your mind with the ability to believe that you can go from searching for a physical father and be restored, to a personal relationship with our Heavenly Father, and become a total **Daddy's Girl**.

Guess What? Here is His Promise to You.

"...I will never leave you nor forsake you."
Hebrews 13:5 NKJV

MAY GOD BLESS YOU!

Table of Contents

Chapter 1 - Abandoned 1

Chapter 2 – The Pains of Rejections 12

Chapter 3 – Looking for Love 19

Chapter 4 – Breached Reputation 29

Chapter 5 – The Hot Chase 38

Chapter 6 – Sins of the Father 42

Chapter 7 – A Message to My Daughter 48

Chapter 8 – Are You a Covergirl? 55

Chapter 9 – Break the Cycle 61

Chapter 10 – Fill the Void 66

Chapter 11 – Detox Time 73

Chapter 12 – Redeeming the Time 82

References 84

CHAPTER 1

ABANDONED

"As a father is kind to his children, so the LORD is kind to those who honor him."
Psalm 103:13 GNT

I grew up in Philadelphia, Pennsylvania, Carmella D. Chandler. I have a twin brother, we are fraternal twins and we lived in a beautiful neighborhood, had a great church family and great parents. We went to Christian school in Willow Grove, which was all white at that time, until my twin and I got there.

I Had a Dream Home

Five years later, my sister arrived, then another brother a year later. I will be the first to admit, as little children you get a little jealous when another sibling comes on the scene. Being too young to grasp the feeling and not really knowing what it means, but now I know, these new siblings were taking my daddy's attention that I always wanted. There were more of us now and he had to divide his attention among us all, I just didn't like it, I wanted my daddy time all to myself.

What can a girl ask for? I had the dream, both of my parents, being raised in the Christian life, family time, and so much more. When my Dad came through the door after a hard day's work, he would sit for a minute to unwind and play his guitar. How cool was that? Smooth handsome and fun loving always made me laugh. When we would go to church he would play in a group and I remember having a feeling of pride, thinking, "That's my dad."

My Dream Was Interrupted and I Had to Wake Up

Well, do you know how you feel when you wake up from a dream, and it was good but interrupted? That's what happened to me, my dream was shattered. I never expected that I would be suddenly awakened to the reality of the pains of human existence at such an early age. I was nine years old, and I will never forget the day, that daddy left. Words fail me to describe the incorrigible feeling of rejection and desolation that came over me. Little did I know that the incessant arguments, cold responses and loud silence that existed in our home was a bomb, ticking to explode. My parents were going through a divorce.

Although, they tried to veil the ugly situation, but soon the 'beast' was let out of the bag. It seemed at the time the world came crashing down on 'little' me. You would have thought that my Daddy had actually passed away; at least, that was how it felt to me.

Like a Broken Cistern...

Life became too hard and unbearable. According to my mom, I acted out for a long time. In fact, it got so serious that I had to see a professional psychotherapist due to issues about my deviant behavior.

Today, as I look back at those times, I feel things should have happened differently. My thoughts and feelings were running so wild and there was an ugly scenario that keeps playing out in my mind. I remember actually yelling out in deep hurt and frustration to my mom, "What did you do?", "Why did you let him go!!!" I felt as though it was all her fault that my Daddy was gone. I blamed her for everything. I believed that she could have stopped Daddy from leaving or she must have done something that pushed him away from us.

My Daddy was so important to me that when he left, it felt like a layer of skin was torn off my chest. How could this have happened? I never saw it coming. I was devastated. I needed my Daddy.

For the First Time I Felt.... Abandoned

I was feeling so abandoned and got lost in the maze of depression, frustration, unworthiness and endless questions. The feeling of being deserted, cast off and forsaken came over me. Yes, this is what it means to be "abandoned" and I was increasingly allowing these feelings to overtake me deeper and deeper as the days went by.

It became difficult to do anything because all I wanted was my Daddy to come back. I felt as though he left me and I longed so much for him to come back home.

I Had to Grow Up Quickly to Survive

In Brother Paul's letter to the Corinthians, there was a part where he made profound affirmation. He said in 1 Corinthians 13:11 NKJV, "When I was a child, I used to speak as a child, I understood as a child, I thought as a child; but when I become a man, I put away childish things."

I have come to realize that, our ability to adapt to conditions and situations around us is a key element of growth and survival in all the ages of human existence. It quickly dawned on me that I had to fight to survive. I went through a season of perpetual test and mandatory growth. The truth is the 'little girl' that I was, no longer had to remain the same, she had to 'grow up.'

Even though I had my mother, I couldn't even imagine the road ahead for her raising four children on her own. There was no one to help, we had to look after ourselves. We were faced with the harsh reality of the fact that Daddy was gone! Every day was a reminder of the cruelty of some of life's realities.

Unfortunately, Today, The Ugly Stats are Rising...

I want to take a moment to point your attention to striking statistics about "Daddy's issues" in America. According to the U.S. Census Bureau, the share of children living in mother-only households has risen from eight percent in 1960 to twenty-three percent in 2010. The role parents play in the lives of their children, are obviously important.

What if 'Daddies' were Around?

Past research has shown that a father's involvement with his children is linked to all kinds of beneficial outcomes; from higher academic achievement, improved social and emotional well-being, to lower incidences of delinquency, risk taking, and other problem behaviors.

Although this is according to the census bureau, it does not look into the reality of being a single parent. Unfortunately, children are being exposed to many harmful situations and experiences that they should never have to experience or go through.

We Were Vulnerable

There is joy, peace and security when children grow up in a loving atmosphere and under the two-watchful eyes of a caring father and affectionate mother. Unfortunately, I am a survivor of the negative impact of "Fatherlessness." Daddy's absence almost ruined our lives. My Mom couldn't be with us all the time so, my siblings and I had to sometimes go to babysitters and the caretakers.

We sometimes had to stay with babysitters who had older sons. Thankfully, I was never raped; however, people took advantage of us and our situation. You can only imagine the abuse and exploitation that came with Daddy's absence. I experienced fondling and masturbation at a young age and I didn't really know the difference between 'bad' touch and an 'appropriate' touch.

We Went Through Episodes of Pain and Trauma…

Today, I look back with a tinge of sorrow and I ask, "Why life should turn out so cold and cruel?" Our vulnerability was harshly exploited by people who dragged us through series of traumatic experiences.

I vividly remember an incident when someone broke into our home. My Mom tried all she could to defend herself but her strength was no match, so she called on the name of Jesus and the assailant immediately jumped up and ran out. It was like someone knew my father was no longer around and the door was left wide open and we were an easy prey.

> *...Do not be terrified or dismayed (intimidated), for the LORD your God is with you wherever you go.*
> *Joshua 1:9 AMP*

Consequently, I almost drowned in an unending flow of tears when I saw my mother in agony and pain after this attack. Once again, I asked, "Why???" I cried often during my teen years, because we had no protector and because my dad was not around. No one was there to stand up for us or shield us from hurt and pain.

I Resorted to Prayer and Turned to God...

What do you do when you are faced with daunting situations? Thankfully, I knew the power of prayer at a young age. Many times, I find peace in pouring my heart to God. It seemed like the only way through the storms in my life. I would say, "Jesus, help me, bring my Daddy back. What more could I ask for?"

Other times, I expressed myself in poems and as I was writing and crying, this is what came to me.

Why?
I was Fatherless and I ask the question why?
It was not enough to see you in a suit and tie,
My my my, I'm about to cry!
With tears flowing from my eyes,
"Was I not good enough?"
I thought and prayed
I guess not cuz you would have stayed
Time and time again I would search within,
Did I do something wrong? Did I sin?
I did everything I could to get you on the phone,
to see what I could do to bring you back home,
but it was too late I was almost grown.
As years gone by, I thought let's give it a try to heal
the hurt and the wounds and ask the question why?
What happened Daddy? Why didn't you stay?
You wouldn't understand baby girl just begin to pray.
I did that already as I begin sigh,
give me the answer tell me the reason why?

Maybe when you're older you will begin to understand,
it's hard out here to be a young man.
I have four young children to dress and feed,
So, listen carefully and take heed
I was young and full of life,
And now I have four kids and a wife.
Please understand this was not the plan,
Did I just tell you I was just a young man?
When you're in your 20s it's all fresh and new,
Then your mom gave birth to the two of you.
I was excited a boy and a girl.
This change my whole world.
Again, let me say this as I begin to sigh,
"Do you still want to know the real reason why?"
Well I don't have all the answers as I search within,
But I do know it started with a three-letter word **SIN**.

---

*"His leaving wasn't about you;
it was about him."*
-Iyanla Vanzant

CHAPTER 2

THE PAINS OF REJECTION

...so will I be with you; I will not fail you or abandon you.
Joshua 1:5 AMP

A Little about My Moral Background

When I was about to graduate high school at 17 years old and preparing to go to college, everything was 'Peachy-keen' [you know what I mean].

We have been in Mt. Sinai Church since when I was 14 years old and the church background was a great influence on my mom and how she raised me and my siblings. When I was younger, I used to think that my mom was 'Old school,' but now I realize that she was raising us with the foundation of the church and Christian principles.

Interestingly, when it comes to allowing me relate with boys, my Momma was always cautious and overly sensitive. This was why she always insisted that my twin brother must go with me on dates. I know you are thinking, what a "funny idea!" Of course, that never went over well with the boy or his parents for that matter.

I still recall a funny incident when a boy from the school asked me out on a date to senior prom. This time again, my mother wanted to talked to the parents, and she gave the 'run-down' of questions that maybe another mother wouldn't have expected. She asked, "Is he saved? Sanctified? Holy Ghost filled? What church do you attend?" Well, needless to say I didn't go to the prom with him!

Regrettably, a lot of girls I knew already had experience with sex, and this eventually turned out to be a negative influence in my life. Often times, I was teased and the peer pressure got to me, but I stuck to the values my mother was teaching us. Kids can be so cruel, they told me that boys didn't like me and didn't want to be with me because I wasn't giving it up.

I remember one sad experience when I got back to school, because I wasn't going to the prom with this boy. He ended up spreading terrible rumors about me. The news got around fast, he told others that "he hit it!" and he was taking someone else.

I couldn't easily explain the hurt that I experienced, the lie, the rejection, the smeared reputation? I felt like I should run home and cry on my daddy's shoulder maybe it would ease my pain. Daddy would have said, "Who hurt you, baby, what's his name?"

Well thank God for church family. One of the ministers we talked to in a teen group discussed situations where pride or male ego just gets in the way. They try to impress their boys, just to look like they got a notch on their belt and it doesn't matter who they hurt and the devastating implications of their actions.

1 Searched for Love at an Early Age

Affectionate relationships are a vital element of human existence. Naturally, the desire to be loved always grows stronger when we experience rejection. It is always an agonizing experience. A child who is loved and adored by his or her parents may not yet appropriately appreciate what he or she has been blessed with. However, the reality is, we sometimes don't fully appreciate what we have until it's lost.

When I think about my friends and classmates who were exposed to sexual relationships at an early age, I wonder what was so special about this 'fleeting' pleasure.' I didn't get the memo at all… Still can't understand why anyone would risk losing so much for so little! I mean the experience was over before you could say, "Ouch!"

However, after what seemed like a cut in my flesh, I began to feel the pain of separation from my "Father's love." I needed to fill the void of the affection and love that I have always enjoyed. So, I began an unending search for a "cure-all or solution" for the "pains of rejection" that lingered with me for a long time. I thought getting married young would fulfill all my daddy issues. Of course, the love, hugs, and companionship would complete me. Right? Well, No! It turned out to be an entirely wrong idea!

In Search of a Surrogate

In the society, it is commonly accepted that, 'fatherless' girls often tend to idealize their absent fathers. Consequently, they view other men in their lives through rose-tinted glasses. This is why, they ask unending questions like: "Does he talk like Daddy? How about his appearance and mannerism? Does he even play like Daddy?" However, little do they realize that, they are naturally inclined to relate with men who take after Daddy.

To validate this idea, Kerry Daynes, a Psychologist based in Manchester affirmed that, "There is a wealth of evidence to show that women are attracted to men who bear more than a passing resemblance of their fathers, whether in behavior, personality or looks." He explained that, "There's a critical period during childhood, when a girl imprints upon herself, the traits and characteristics of her father and carries these into adult life. However, one thing we need to realize is, this can turn out to be a lasting 'blessing' or a serious 'mistake'."

Fathers Are Reflections of Our Life's Expectation...

For instance, a girl who had been acquainted with the love, attention, care, and quality time with her father would easily get attracted to a man who shows similar traits and characteristics. Even more, this 'girl' will often consciously or unconsciously expect or demand these traits or qualities from other boys or men in her life. This makes the girl search for a male friend or husband like her father even in adulthood.

Evidently, fathers are the 'eyes' through which their children see. This is why, they play a very important role in their daughter's life choices, attitudes and expectations which in-turn reflect in their degree of happiness, well-being and overall life experience.

Furthermore, fathers have a direct impact on the lives of their daughters. Whatever the girl knows about the masculine gender begins from what she knows about her father. You see, girls first learn how the male gender behaves, react and do things from their dad at home. On the long run, it becomes easier for them to understand the emotional, physical, psychological and mental language of men. Again, this 'knowledge' can be sometimes useful and at other times very 'biased', especially if the girl was raised by a father who was a negative influence.

Therefore, a girl-child should be able to learn from her father, first-hand, about her worth, identity, how to be treated, loved and cherished. This is because, a father is his child's first and primary model, who provides him/her with a blue print of what to expect when they are all grown up.

CHAPTER 3

LOOKING FOR LOVE

We relate to all other men base on what we experienced with our father first.
-Dr. Michelle Watson

How do you know that you have a void to be filled, if you don't know what needs to be in that space that is so empty? Well I guess I'm about to find out.

If I ever needed a Dad's counsel, it was at this time! I threw myself into church activities, started working and at the same time attending college. Before I knew it, I realized I had turned 18 years old. That age seems like the focal point of transformation, you either can bend negatively or positively depending on how you are able to adequately control the newly ushered in privileges.

I moved and lived by myself in an apartment that my mom had purchased. It was being renovated when I moved in, but it was my own space. I thought wow how many 18-year-olds have their own place, paying rent, utilities, and buying their own food? Indeed! It felt great! Enough privacy, no curfew, no sister sharing a room with you, and practically owe no one an explanation for the decisions you make. It felt really good!

I quickly realized that not only did I think it was cool, but so did my friends. I was asked to throw a party, that's what teens do, right? Also, after much pressure from friends, I thought of giving smoking or drinking a fair try. Yuck! Quite as expected, that didn't last a day. This is where the upbringing that my mother instilled in me paid off. I knew right from wrong and it was very difficult to shed my skin and become wild. The word says, "Train up a child in the way it should go and when they grow old, they will not depart from it." (Proverbs 22:6). Trust me, Mama raised me right!

Of course, living independently didn't go down well with my pastor, as well as my father. When my father heard about it and it was quite unsettling and I still had my questions hanging in thin air. I could never really shake the fact that my father left and during pivotal times in my life, I would often feel like history was about to repeat itself in the worse way possible.

However, I met someone at a church convention. My friends and cousins knew that I was like an old school kind of girl and even their parents knew I was a good influence on them. As a result, they loved having me around.

While hanging out in the lobby, waiting for the service to start, we were too excited about the attention my girlfriends and I were getting from the males. One of my friends was approached by a guy who asked about me. She told him bluntly that he would only be wasting his time if he tried and he was having a wrong perception of me.

Somehow, it seemed like her response challenged his ego. That egoistic feeling men have when someone had just challenged their ability to undergo a task rose up in him. But, like the saying, "curiosity killed the cat." Well, I was about to find out how true the saying was.

People often say, daughters with an absentee father tend to over compensate to be liked or accepted. They don't want to feel the sting of rejection from a male so they do all they can to be liked even if they have to sometimes act stupid or excessive.

Again, I had a very wrong mindset. I thought of every guy I met as a husband material. Each time, I felt this was going to be the man to fill in the gaps left by my absent father. Time would indicate that I was certainly wrong.

I vividly remember that, my parents, married at a very young age, and always kept saying "marriage is honorable," and of course, "no sex before marriage." After they married, they gave birth to me and my twin brother. I began to think to myself, "Is this my destiny too? Would I like to have this kind of future?"

As he approached me, my nerves kept whispering tingles to each other. As young women, it seemed it's almost embedded in us to pretend and act like we don't have interest in whatever a man who's wooing us says. Most times, we don't want them having the impression of us being easy, so we play hard to get. I tried to but for some reason I developed an attraction to almost every guy that paid me attention. Here is another alibi for my broken heart... So, I thought, like I always do..."Can this be him?"

Why Do Good Girls Love Bad Boys?

At this juncture I need to talk a little about the reason for the enigma, "Why good girls love bad boys." The reality is, bad boys have the reputation of hot, good looking, scruffy, arrogant, inconsiderate; but also, cocky, inattentive and almost unfeeling.... Yet women flock around them.

Research has proved that many times a young woman who have a desire to date a bad boy had issues tracing back to their father. According to Carole Lieberman, M. D. Clinical Psychiatry, "The main reason women are attracted to bad boys is because of the relationship they had with their fathers, when they were little girls that made them feel unlovable, not good enough, to attract a prince. Therefore, they end up kissing many frogs.

However, other issues played a part, underlying most issues if they idealized what a father's role played in their upbringing /challenges in their daddy issues."

Now Back to My Story

Carelessly, I hopped from one romantic relationship to the other. Sadly, onetime, I was dumped, I was so devastated. It felt like I lost my self-worth. As time went by, I gradually but painfully came to realize that relationships with 'boys' offers no relief and oftentimes complicates everything, making things worse. I had to change my focus.

I came to a stage in my life where I knew I had to make some changes. I began to focus on the better things of life. I began to see things improve in my situation and I got a better understanding and serious meaning of what my life was to be. Then, I met someone that was in the church, active, his parents and family also attended the church frequently. Everything seemed nice and good. And yes, I was enthusiastic and really excited about how the next episode was going to unfold. Things had turned around and my focus had changed.

In 1 Peter 5:8 it says, 'Be sober, be vigilant; because your adversary the devil, as a roaring lion, walked about, seeking whom he may devour." I guess I wasn't in any way vigilant neither was I sober, the opposite of both had firm grip on me. All the right words were spoken to me, and all the right moves and actions were made. I met the family, worshipped with family in the same church. Things seemed to be great, but it lasted only eight months then it was all over. Yes, I meant practically over! Why? Well, simply because I gave up the cookie.

Truthfully, those few seconds of 'pleasure' turn out to be a mirage. I got nothing but more years of pain. I was filled with more emptiness and void which had a long-term effect on me. Often, I think to myself, "Wow! What was all the 'hype' about?" I was looking for love in all the wrong places, when really all I needed was the affection and love of my Daddy.

"The Role of a Father is to teach his daughter how to be in a non-sexual relationship with a man."
-Iyanla Vanzant

Buried but Not Dead

There is always a fresh uncovering, like scales falling from your eyes when you've just gone through a hot served round of despair or disappointment. You then have a keen urge to do something great and right to appease or rather, console yourself after despair, loss or disappointment. Well, I decided to move on and bury my hurts, pains, and whys. I decided to keep myself-busy in reading books and gaining fresh insights. I had a great job at the hospital and at the church as well. My daily routine became more predictable.

However, after a while, it seemed as if I was not moving fast enough in getting on with my life, I was more focused on myself than having any thought or consideration for anyone else. So, my mom introduced me to her best friend's son. Although I expressed to him that I was not ready to date, surprisingly he was fine just being friends. And it was exactly that way, for months. He talked about the word of

God, read a lot, and loved to talk. I got thinking of him as being different from any other man I've met.

Right now, I'm 19 years old and he's 22. I was asked to visit his church a few times and of course I went. We got along well and I could sense this seemed like a start of something beautiful, like a fairytale. Everything looked right. He was a perfect gentleman and had introduced me to his family and friends. And then……it happened!

CHAPTER 4

BREACHED REPUTATION

I Ran into a Season of Despair and Shame...

Although, I had a diligent, loving, caring, confident and beautiful mother, yet, I felt the harsh consequences of my Daddy's absence in my life. The implications of his absence were far-reaching. I didn't enjoy the natural benefits of a father's affection, counsel, company and comfort. I had to thrive, survive and navigate through the storms of life virtually alone, without a "Father's support."

As a result of this, I fell into the trap of getting pregnant at an early age. I was ashamed of myself and confused about what to do. As if that was not enough, the pressure to get married started to weigh me down. This was because one thing my mother always emphasized was that, "It's better to marry then to burn."

"But if they cannot contain, let them marry."
                        1 Corinthians 7:9 KJV

How could this have happened to me? I use to feel so proud of myself that, I was being a good girl with my 'virginity' intact. I never saw this coming.

I began to receive so many counsels from people, including some people who had tremendous influence on me. Some of them advised that, I needed to save myself from the shame of having a baby outside wedlock. This meant that, I should get married, before my belly becomes protruded and my pregnancy starts to show.

While this advice sounded good at that time, today, I am wiser and I knew better than this. Marriage is not meant to be used as a cloak to cover reproach or a refuge from shame; rather, it is a sacred institution built on integrity, trust, understanding and sincerity.

Moreover, before you think that, I had all the wrong advice, think again, there is more. Since I belonged in a "Christian-circle," marriage would have saved me the embarrassment of having to carry a pregnancy outside wedlock. However, I was shock to my very core, to get some advice that suggested aborting my baby to cover my mistake with an innocent child's blood and lazily sweep my error under the carpet of cruelty.

Certainly, I knew that I wasn't going to continue this terrible act. You see, getting married will always be a better alternative to abortion. To drive home this cruel advice, I still remember what one of them said to me, she said, "Even if you are in the second trimester of this pregnancy, it doesn't matter you still have time to terminate this pregnancy and you need to act fast!"

At This Point, I Became So Confused and Afraid...

I was really confused because I knew that some girls around me were actually getting pregnant but having abortions to conceal their shame. Needless-to-say I had to listen to all of those advices and obviously I needed help. Yet, I found none, I felt alone, nervous and afraid.

The cause of my fear and anxiety were not far-fetched. I was the 'poster-child' of virginity. I mean someone who goes to church and invites other teens to church as well. The news about my pregnancy was clearly not to be heard. How would it sound to the ears of the other teens? What would I say to justify myself? Who would trust me anymore after they hear that I got pregnant?

This led to episodes of depression and heartache. I felt so much regret, shame and guilt. I wanted an escape from my predicament. I wish I had a chance to start all over again. However, with every passing day, the reality of my predicament dawned on me even more and more.

I Had to Let the Cat Out of the Bag…Ugly but Expected

I never imagined that, my craving for love and acceptance would plunge me deeper into uglier situations. After I suffered from the pains of rejection and neglect from my Daddy all I wanted was to find peace and comfort. I just wanted to be loved, accepted and valued. I felt having a boyfriend was going to get me what I desperately needed. Also, there is that deep desire to 'fit-in.' No one really wants to be an out-cast or the odd one out. Everyone was doing it, so I felt I should try it! I wanted to be just like the other girls.

Well, finally, I couldn't just keep this to myself anymore. I needed to tell my Dad. I knew this was not going to go all well. I felt I had to tell him because deep down inside I thought this was entirely his fault.

All those questions I had before came rushing back. I began to ask, "Where was he when I desperately needed him? How can he blame me for seeking out what he had deprived me of? How did he expect me to cope with his absence?"

Since Daddy had not been with us, he has little or no blame to cast on me, I had to survive. I felt that a girl of nineteen years old should be independent and able to thrive on her own. These were the thoughts racing through my 'naïve mind' and I finally got the confidence that I needed to tell him my secret, that I was pregnant.

I Felt Telling Dad Should Not be that Difficult

You never know what to expect when it comes to Daddy! He is often full of surprises. This played out again! Aside from the fact that, I felt a quite justified thinking that, Daddy should not put all the blame on me for my situation, yet I doubted if he wouldn't be too hard on me. My anxiety subsided a little after speaking with my pastor and his wife. The response I received from them was, "You aren't the first and you won't be the last." They didn't condemn me, so that boosted my confidence enough to tell Daddy.

When I spoke with Daddy, it sure did not go the way I had expected nor anticipated. He was so upset, to say the least. I really felt that he didn't have anything to say to me because he left us! Daddy left us unsupervised, unprotected, vulnerable and uncovered! I didn't understand why he was so angry, he left us, so why is he now starting to care. He should have cared enough to stay. All through these times, I felt vulnerable like open prey. As other men came into my life, they could can see or sense that there was not a male presence around. Some know how I hungered for their attention, but the attention I received was not for my gratification, but theirs. See, if you are a person with low self-esteem and you desire to be showered with love and acceptance you become susceptible to preying men. I fell right into the trap of these preying men and now realize it was not a good place for me or anyone to be in.

To explain this natural inclination, someone said, "A daughter should not have to beg her father for [love or] relationship [It should be freely made available to her]."

Unfortunately, this chase kept me on the wrong road of negative thought pattern and perception as regards relationships. Come to think of it, I was supposed to be the 'princess' and should have been shown first-hand how to be treated by a man by my Daddy. Instead, I just idealize these things in my almost 'clueless' mind.

Consequently, I had to come up with what a male figure in my life would look like. This led me to series of eventful experimentation with relationships with the opposite sex. So, I began to date.

As expected, since I grew up in the church, I knew all too well about waiting for marriage before having sex but the problem was despite my church background, I was still a little naïve. Besides being naïve, I just wanted to be loved by a man to fill the void of not having my father in my life.

If I couldn't have him, I got to the point where I thought just having a man, any man in my life would fulfill these deep deficiencies in my life. I couldn't have been more wrong and had to live with the consequences of my decisions.

CHAPTER 5

THE HOT CHASE

Caught in a Glance at a Reflection of My Heart's Deep Desire

For the next seven years, I kept up this role of pursuer. I was chasing something, but nothing satisfied me. I just wanted to know the truth. Questions kept coming to me. I often asked, "Why? Why did things have to go the way they did? Why couldn't we stay a family? Why did Daddy have to leave? Why was I not good enough for you to stay? Why did I let him go in the first place? Why? Why? Why?" All these questions and always the same answer, "You are too young to understand."

As much as I wanted the truth, I knew that pointing the accusatory finger and playing the blame game was not the answer or proper way to handle the situation. We will not only stop any progress, but we will not get to the bottom of the situation. We will remain in a perpetual loop of questions and feelings of hurt, rejection and abandonment. The only source we can gain a true understanding is to turn our situation over to God. The longer we search and delay in turning to God for answers, then our search will continue forever. He has the answers. They may not be what we want to hear, but they are truly what we need to hear.

The void and emptiness that fatherlessness created in me was almost unbearable. To no avail, I continued to chase *after* my Daddy's love. I employed several creative ways to meet up with him either after school, at his job, or home. Anyway, just to get time with Daddy. The more I spent time with him, the "why-questions" began to not bombard my thoughts as much and they would not play over and again in my mind.

What You Don't Know Will Hurt You

This may seem like a shock to men, but the reality is, contrary to popular belief, children do not care about child support or monetary gifts, all they want is Daddy's time and his presence. Evidently, there is no amount of money in the world that can replace one thing you desire to get back the most, the time lost by not being there. The reality is, every relationship is nourished or starved to the degree of the time invested in it.

I wonder why boys and men keep playing their silly game. The games that primarily consist of "pursue and conquer, then evade." Interestingly, nice but naïve girls often fall for their game and end up hurt and damaged.

The truth is, the adult phase of my life wouldn't have been so bad, had I got sound and sincere "Fatherly advice." I had received advice from different men; however, it was bad advice. Some of this bad advice even came from those in leadership. For instance, I was told by a 'Pastor' that, "You are too independent and no man will want you." He continued by saying, "If you can do it all by yourself, so what? Do you really want a man?"

Advice like this is what formed my biased perception about relationships and men generally. I leaned an important lesson in discernment. I learned that it is critical to discern what is of the flesh and what is of the spirit while receiving advice from anyone offering it.

CHAPTER 6

SINS OF THE FATHER

"Thou shalt not bow down thyself to them, nor serve them: for I the Lord thy God am a jealous God, visiting the iniquity of the fathers upon the third and fourth generation children unto them that hate me." - **Exodus 20:5 KJV**

Isn't it the responsibility of every parent to ensure they tread carefully on their path through life so that their innocent children don't fall victims of mistakes they had themselves made?

Well, of course, the first time I got pregnant it did not go too well, especially in the church and while I decided to keep my baby, others decided not to keep theirs. If I had listened to the numerous voices of people that echoed negatively in my ears, perhaps my beautiful daughter would not have been here today. I may have been young and naïve about a lot of things, yet I had the fear God at heart. I never considered the option of aborting my baby. I chose to go through the shame, timidity, and hate comments from people than commit the murder of an innocent child who hadn't commit any crime. This was my baby and even though I didn't plan for her to come, God did and he has a purpose for this life he placed within me. So, I couldn't end that life that was not even an option for me.

My decision to keep my baby lead to many giving me their strongly opinionated advice. This advice came coupled with the fear and pressure to marry the father because I was pregnant. So, I decided to get married.

I was both angry and confused at the same time. While some were pushing me to get married, my father was saying something completely different. When I spoke to my father, he told me not to do it. Bluntly, he said, "Just because you made a mistake, doesn't mean you should hurry into another. Do not add getting married to the equation." Surprisingly, my Pastor offered a similar advice to me.

There's a saying that says, "When two or more people strike on the same point it more likely gains more attention." Actually, it felt wrong to force something that was not playing out naturally. I had become more mature and thought to myself that I could actually handle raising a baby on my own. But I also had to think about him, was he prepared to be a husband and a father. Then, it hit me! This was history on the verge of repeating itself. Am I in the same situation my parents were in? Did my situation just answer some of those "why" questions I had for so long? I was at the same age when my parents got married and pregnant. What a coincidence?

Remember, it is said that, it's only natural to fall for a man similar to your father, not so much in their actions, but their traits or personality. Of course, you don't go out purposely to find that, but it seemed like second nature. For me this was true almost all the time. I didn't realize that the men I dated had birthdays almost the same and date or close. Their character and how I was treated also mimicked that of how my father treated me. I began to notice a striking trend and consistent similarity.

Oh! How I wish I could wake up only to realize this was all a dream, just a really, really bad dream, but it wasn't. Steve Harvey said that "Life is 10 percent of what happens to you and 90 percent what you're going to do about it." I realized that, I can do something about all I had been through. After all, with God all things are possible if we just believe. Life has given me some curve balls, but I decide to go with it, and learn from it. That's the key right? It is funny how when we try not to repeat a matter it just keeps coming back around.

I felt like Paul when he said, in Romans 7:19 KJV, "For the good that I would I do not: but the evil which I would not, that I do." What does that mean?

Finally, I Got Married!

So, now, it begins, my life with a husband and baby. How did I get here? Does this question sound familiar to anyone? I believe it is more common than we think. At this point, I realize that, I cannot blame anyone but myself.

Why did I blame my Daddy for the emotional hurt, was it a disconnection in some way of him not being there? However, I ought to be responsible for the outcome of my life, not my dad or whatever circumstance I had been through. After all, he won't stand alongside me to give account of how I had lived my life. I am responsible for doing that and for my own actions.

Sometimes, you get tired of all the rant of whose fault it is in divorced parents, it weighs very heavy on you and the thought of choosing sides. I really thought if I had pursued my father and got his attention in some way he could have come back home. I thought with so many weird events happening in our life that he would want to come back and see about us. Perhaps, I was wrong! And maybe, just maybe they were some things I just was too young to understand.

CHAPTER 7

A MESSAGE TO MY DAUGHTER

There are many daughters in this world, who are going through there Daddy issues. Yes, I started out bitter in the beginning because I was in my healing and recovery stage. I began to be arrested in my spirit and this helped me to better understand all that I had endured. As I went through my process, I quickly learned that my story is relatable to millions of girls and woman. As I embraced my personal relationship with the Lord and submitted to growing and maturing in Him, I began to see the importance of this topic for others, not just myself. I still need to stay focus on my healing and overcoming the opposition of the enemy in my thoughts, but I also had to develop a message that will bring healing and deliverance to others.

Even though I made bad choices and decisions and experienced many failed relationships, I needed to get to the root of my issues. I needed to overcome the desire to know why and I needed to start my journey of forgiveness to my father and seek the Heavenly Father to lead me in my healing process.

I made a decision and decided that this cycle must end. My daughter is the next generation affected with Daddy issues; however, this cycle must be broken with her. So that is why I wrote this poem to my daughter.

> **Dear Daughter,**
> *We tend to look for love in all the wrong places,*
> *Because of their sexy and cute smiling faces.*
> *Yeah, they tall dark and handsome,*
> *While holding your soul up for ransom.*
> *Yes, you get caught up in an ugly soul-tie,*
> *Still searching and trying to find the real reason why?*
> *The pain and the hurt are still there,*
> *But do you think that they even care?*
> *So, you get caught up in a vicious cycle,*

While held up in a room with a dude named Michael
Yeah you still running place to place,
While looking for love and trying to save face!
Well I think I have the problem solved,
And it concerns all who's involved!
There is a man who is dying to meet you,
And he has a record to be tried and true.
His name is Jesus!
Yeah, I know you heard of Him,
He is different and He's not like the rest of them.
Girl let me tell you and hand you a box of tissues,
Because He healed and delivered me out of all my Daddy issues.

I have seen first-hand what not having a father figure can do in a girl's life. As I received my healing and deliverance, I then was able to see the same patterns in others' lives. I was able to see their brokenness from the same issues I experienced. The young girls and women experiencing these issues no longer need to be broken, but this heaviness is what needs to be broken, but how do we do that? When you see a woman, whether she is a mother, grandmother, aunt, sister, niece, cousin; and the common link is not blood, but the Daddy issue, reach out to her. We all know someone or have personally experienced it ourselves and have been touched or effective by fatherlessness in some form or another. It is said that, if fatherlessness was a disease, it would be considered an epidemic. That's just how big of a problem we are facing in this day and time.

Even in myself, I started to see some traits that were not good at first such as having a low self-esteem and the intense feelings of being rejected, being used or mistreated. I became a people pleaser, while trying to find my way and trying to fit in. The next trap I fell into was when I began to belittle myself or dummy down and compromise my values.

None of this made me happy, it actually did the opposite. Once I began to compromise my values, I felt terrible and remorse because I was going against the Christian values my mother had placed in my life. Also, it did not bring me the friends I was looking for, it didn't bring me the man I was looking for and it didn't bring my Daddy back. So, then I felt like my efforts were in vain and no matter what I did, nothing was going to work. This opened the door for depression to come in and hinder my life even more.

Now that I look back and reflect, I have to ask myself, "Was it worth it?" I can now honestly answer that question and say, "No way!" I can now refocus my attention to the things that matter and use my testimony as a tool to help others from falling prey to the same traps that placed me in bondage and created strongholds in my life.

Please Acknowledge

At some point in our lives we will have to acknowledge where we are, so you may not have had your physical or biological father around, and that is alright. We have to find peace in our hearts and minds then begin to confess and release them. Unfortunately, we cannot deny or confess that we don't need them or we were fine without them, but the key is to forgive and release them. You have to begin to heal. Don't wait for an apology, because the truth of the matter is you may never get it. Don't do it for them, do it for you! Remember, you cannot change anyone or fix anyone else but yourself. The only man that can change or fix them is God! Don't make yourself crazy trying to do God's job, He can handle it all by Himself.

I have realized I cannot go back and change what happened or how it happened, all I can do is get to the root of my issues and identify and begin to give and submit everything in prayer. I have to surrender my heart and acknowledge that I cannot move forward until I deal with what was holding me back. Sometimes getting to the root is a long process of digging up old feelings in order to properly dealing with them. You may have to unearth some of the very things that have been buried and covered. Oftentimes, it is a painful process, but it's for the good. It's the best route to take because when you just cover something up and don't treat it properly, it won't properly heal. In some cases, it will only fester and get worse. Then years down the road something will trigger you causing you to revisit the pain again. The wound wasn't properly healed, but just covered up. So, invest the time now to uncover and heal properly, utilizing the word of God as your source and guide along with the presence of the Holy Spirit. That is the only way to do it correctly.

CHAPTER 8

ARE YOU A COVERGIRL?

Prayerfully, by the time you get to the end of this chapter you may start to recognize your true self. It's time to get naked and strip away all that is weighing you down. Let's take off all the fake smiles or laughs, all the falsies, the lashes and derma blend. Are you uncovered and bare? You may feel a little awkward, but it's for your good. Bare your all to God and be completely honest with Him regarding the things that are keeping you in bondage. God already sees you and knows everything, but you have to see you and learn who you are. It's time for you to be transparent with yourself. The make-up industries have made billions of dollars from us because we want to be flawless and beautiful, but we are just covering up our outer appearances and neglecting what is within. We are fearfully and wonderfully made from the inside out. Make-up is not going to help with the inside. Make-up is often used to make us look like or be someone we are not. Don't get me wrong there is nothing wrong with make-up or looking and feeling beautiful or feeling young and lively, but physically and spiritually it goes deeper than the products we put on our face and bodies to enhance our features.

Let's look at this in another way. In order to cover and mask ourselves of the blemishes and imperfections we conceal first, and then lay the foundation and blend in. Sounds familiar, right? Believe it or not many of us do this in life, we hide behind the hurt and pain, the rejection and low self-esteem coving up the real issues. I said earlier that when things are covered, they don't heal well. We got so good at covering things up and got so dependent on our favorite product that we forget with what the real issue was until we run out of product. Now you can't leave the house because you don't have your foundation on. You haven't concealed. What am I to do now? We don't want to run into those situations, so we have to face the truth and face the issues.

We have gotten so good at covering up we started to teach tutorials but have not dealt with our own issues. Have you ever been told what goes on in this house stays in this house or you keep things private and deal with it? Are these the right ways to deal with issues? No! Not at all. Like an onion we have layers and layers of hidden and buried trauma. At first glance the onion is good to look at and smell, but then when you start to peel back the layers and as you go deeper you then your eyes start to water and tear up and then those tears begin to flow down your cheek. The effect advances with a more dramatic effect the longer you are cutting that onion. The same can be true with our emotions and if not dealt with properly, our emotions can take over.

I believe that when you expose a wound to air it heals quicker. Remember when mom use too blow on your boo boo and say, "All better?" Well that's what your Heavenly Father wants to do for you and more. He is the great physician, so He will apply the balm oil and heal all of your issues. Jeremiah 46:11, mentions the healing balm of Gilead.

Don't Be A Picker!

Question? Have you ever begun to heal and then as the wound starts to harden or scab over you think your done healing, so you begin to pick at the scab? Only to find that it begins to bleed again! Stop. You don't want to keep going back and healing and bleeding. It's alright to talk about it and pray about it, but don't get yourself worked up venting especially to the wrong person. Actually, the best person to take it all to is God Himself, but if you believe you just need one earthly person to speak with make sure they are really a true God covenant person who really wants to see you fully delivered, completely healed and 100% whole in Christ

Jesus. Be very prayerful on who you choose to help you along your path to wholeness because if you connect with another broken person more damage can be done in your life. In this process, sometimes brokenness attract brokenness and it is easy to get into a soul tie. You can accidently be knitted together with a spirit that wants to keep you in a perpetual loop of the unknown and that person is being controlled by a demonic force to just give you enough comfort, yet speak things that keep your mind wandering and wondering. If a soul-tie is formed and sins are committed (friendships or sexual or vows commitment), remove yourself from that situation immediately and repent of your sins.

Earlier in the book, I stated I use to call my Dad a lot and couldn't get an answer. In the process of the writing and healing, that taking solace in God's word that Jeremiah 33:3 says, "Call to me and I will answer you, and show you great and mighty things, which you do not know." Just knowing that He will answer me when I call out to Him brings me peace, because He is a good Father, He is a protector and a provider. So just know He wants the best for you!

CHAPTER 9

BREAK THE CYCLE

You and I were chosen for such a time as this. Esther could've chosen to just save herself and not listen the people, but she would have been dead if she didn't do what God called her to do. God would have raised up somebody else to do what she was asked and just know that God's purpose will always be completed, with or without you.

What needs to be extracted from you? There is a world waiting for you to be healed so you can help set others free. The enemy would make you feel like you are all alone, but the unfortunately, the world had an abundance of people who have been in turmoil by being wounded, rejected, used, mistreated, and abused. It's time to expose and share so help can come to heal and have others set free. They can be other woman or even young girls and teenagers. The enemy will use anyone, but it's time for all to be healed.

In order to begin being healed of your Daddy issues, you have to know that history does not have to repeat itself. It can start and stop with you by surrendering it all and releasing it to the Heavenly Father. We try so much to fix things that we have no control over. When we get into broken relationships or marriages, we try to fix that other person and we fail to realize we too are broken. There are two people in the relationship and what we're lacking we can't heal one another without the Heavenly Father's assistance.

Unfortunately, when we get into another relationship and you have not dealt with buried or dead issues, they start to fester and can tend to cause problems years later. Festering makes it difficult to heal properly. You may not be able to go back and correct it what was wrong, but you can learn to forgive and receive the healing you need to have a better relationship going forward. It's not fair for your new relationships to have to contend with the memories and hurts of the former relationships.

It's so important to really take time to yourself. Sit quietly to truly examine yourself. Take responsibility for your role in the situation because we can no longer blame others, it takes two to argue. Yes, there was a cause to this turmoil, and yes it did have adverse effects, but we can no longer live in the past or pass blame. We have to truly move forward, walk in forgiveness, take accountability and ownership of some things in our lives while truly allowing God to heal your brokenness. He has all the pieces and He is able to restore you, but you have to let Him. Don't carry these broken pieces into your next relationship.

You may feel like you've messed up and have made the worst mistakes you've ever made. Sometimes, the hardest person to forgive during these hard times is ourselves. We have to learn that God has already forgiven us, He has already taken care of that situation over 2000 years ago, but it is critical that we learn how to become an overcomer and not get stuck so much in our problems that we have difficulties moving on. We have to make forward motion and we have to get fully healed.

What I have learned and from listening to others, it is a process that should not to be taken lightly. In Revelations 12:11 KJV the word says, "And they overcame him by the blood of the lamb and by the word of their testimony; and they love not their lives and to the death." We are called to be overcomers. If Jesus walked this earth and He overcame everything, all His trials and temptation, we too have the ability to overcome.

The same is true with our testimony, what we have been through is not just for us, but a tool to help others who come in our path in the future. We now have been equipped with the strength and endurance to overcome these very hurtful things in life and through Christ. We now have the confidence to share how we came through and are victorious.

Yes, He looked beyond all of our faults and He took care of our needs just like He did for the Samaritan woman in John 4:7. He can do it for us as well. He is the same yesterday, today and forever more. We can make the decision to break the cycle by stop pushing the rewind button, or stop pressing pause, and stop trying to remain on the scene of where it happened, when it happened, and the pure fact that it happened. All these questions do is leave us with questions and always wondering, "Now what do we do?" We can't afford to stay stuck in stagnant, it's time to move forward and press toward the mark of the high calling! Break the cycle and receive your divine healing from the Heavenly Father.

CHAPTER 10

FILL THE VOID

Do you have a void? A void is defined as not valid or useless, worthless, completely empty vacant and unfilled. When people suffer and feel they have a void in their life they oftentimes try their hardest to fill that void. They begin to fill it with people, they want to feel accepted and, in some cases, loved, so they begin to hang around people to feel useful and needed. They may not always be the right people. They also may begin to experiment with new things or habits which could leave them to a life filled with sex, drugs, alcohol, emotional eating, etc. This dependency they now have with these habits are "filling the void" but not healing the root of the matter. These activities tend to make matters worse than better.

Brethren I count not myself to have apprehended: but this one thing I do, forgetting those things which are behind and reaching forward unto those things which are before. - **Philippians 3:13 KJV**

It is now time to move forward make the transition from Fatherlessness to a Daddy's Girl. I know what happened in my own life, but I have also heard so many stories of other women, young adults, and adolescence who have endured the same issues, that I have to speak up and speak about it. I endured so you can be healed. You have to endure so others can be healed. Our parents are major influencers in our lives and we need them, but there are so many different circumstances that cause our families to not look like the Huxtables. How do we forget those things that are behind? How do we just lay it down and move on? It's a process and it takes time, but we know the Heavenly Father who promised, He will never leave us nor for sake us. We can't do this alone because our flesh will fight us. Our own flesh won't let us overcome, but we have to lay it all down and give it to Jesus. We have to make up our mind that we want to be free. We have to cast our cares on Him, for He cares for us, so we need to let Him take over and surrender to Him. We have to do it wholeheartedly.

In John 4, the bible tells the story of the Samaritan woman who had five husbands and even working on a sixth. Her story is so true in today's society and culture, multiple partners. What do you think she was looking for in these men? What are the ladies of today looking for in all these different men? So many are looking for love, looking for companionship, looking for a fairytale story like Cinderella. In actuality, she is looking for love in all the wrong places. She was looking to fill a void. I suspect she was empty inside and felt unwanted or she felt she wasn't popular or wasn't liked. When you feel a void, you're searching for satisfaction. None of these men filled to void so she moved on from one man to the next and from one relationship to the next, still searching.

Later in the book of John, you will find that her search was over. She finally has an encounter a man that changed her life forever, that man's name is Jesus. Jesus came on the scene and asked a question, "Do you want to be filled with this water? This water I have for you, you will never thirst again. The supply is eternal."

In the Samaritan's story we see that she was in a pattern of broken relationships. Like her, we too keep going back to the similar situations in life because of familiarity. Until we are healed, we end up in the same spot, reaching out to the same source and we are getting the same empty results. Causing us to continually search for something that was never there in the first place. We want new, but we end up in a place that is familiar and the void is still prevalent in our lives. We still feel something is missing, still have that dry empty feeling and don't even know what it is that will quench it, so that is why we are running from place to place, from relationship to relationship.

Let's look at this example that Lord showed me. You have a vase, a bottle, a bucket, and a canteen; but if you're not using the right resource or the right container for what you need, you are going to still be running back to have it filled up. If you're searching for companionship, love and acceptance; the good feelings may only last while the attention is on you, but when the attention shifts, it's time to find those feelings in someone else and be restored with those feelings. In the story of the Samaritan, she found a source that was everlasting and she didn't have to go to various sources any longer, but to the main source and she became refreshed and delighted in what it is she received.

Can you imagine in the 21st Century, you know how they have Jesus pictured in stories and movies with blond hair, blue eyes a goatee, oh my! So here He is sitting at the well waiting on you. Finally, you come and see this man and of course you are in the flesh, you're not looking or thinking of nothing spiritual. You're looking at Him in the flesh, but it's Jesus who came to give us life and give it to us more abundantly. You allow Him to fill you up with His Spirit, fill you up with His love, and fill you up with His peace, allowing Him to give you beauty for your ashes and trading your mourning into laughter. He has now made every crooked place in your life straight and every rough place smooth. Just like the woman at the well, you too need to surrender your life to Him and allow Him to fill you up. Knowing Him will help you to fill the void in your life and put an end to the endless searching and pain you have been putting yourself through.

Prayer to Break Free!

Dear Heavenly Father, we break and release ourselves from the curses on both sides of our family and go back 60 generations. We break every unhealthy soul tie, every unhealthy relationship, and everything that has tried to keep us from our purpose and our destiny. We release ourselves from hurt and unhealthy relationships and unhealthy habits. We surrender it now in the Name of Jesus. We break and release ourselves from all curses of confusion. We break and release ourselves from all self-inflicted words, all negative words we spoke over ourselves and we cancel it right now in the Name of Jesus. We render it null and void in our lives and we thank you right now for expunging our record with you. We thank you for your grace and mercy, we thank you for your forgiveness and we ask you to help us to forgive ourselves. In the mighty Name of Jesus, I pray, Amen!

CHAPTER 11

DETOX TIME

"Therefore, since we are surrounded by such a huge crowd of witnesses to the life of faith, let us strip off every weight that slows us down, especially the sin that so easily trips us up. And let us run with endurance the race God has set before us."
Hebrews 12:1 NLT

The best way to endure the race is by keeping our eyes on Jesus, the champion who initiates and perfects our faith. It's hard enough to run a race or even jog carrying extra stuff. When you're carrying hurts of the past along with shame and guilt, feelings of rejection, low self-esteem, and condemnation; you will be too weighed down to run your race efficiently and effectively causing you to get winded and tired easily. It's time to loose it and let it go.

If Jesus called you to run a race, He wants you to win. He wants you to be victorious. Because in Him we are victorious and more than conquerors. Jesus is our source. It's time to release that old stuff; those offenses, the bitterness, the heartache, the rejection, the addictions, the habits and anything that is coming between you and your savior, Jesus Christ.

Someone leaving or not being in your life as a child is not your fault. Even as an adult if someone leaves your life and it is your fault, ask for forgiveness, both from that person and from yourself. Ask God to help you forgive and ask Him for His forgiveness.

The hard truth is that you may blame the actions of others for the person you became, but at the end of the day we have all made decisions that developed us into who we really are. We had several opportunities to choose right from wrong and the choices we made, set us on our own individual journeys. We may have made some wrong decisions in life, but there is solution! Let's explore this solution in a little more detail.

Everyone may be familiar with fasting and even prayer also meditating on God's word. Believe it or not, fasting removes more than the toxins that have entered your life, but it's a healing process. It is not just for you; it is for other people as well. It releases pride, bitterness, health problems, and deep-seeded issues of hurts. Once it removes those things, your inner man also referred to as your spirit man, will begin to have dominion. Your system will be purged, your mind will be regulated, your emotions will come into subjection of the Holy Spirit and those toxins will be released. The process of purification is taking place and all bad things are being removed from you and being filled with the Holy Spirit. All those things that were keeping you sick and ailing in your body are now being removed and revived, you are being resuscitated by the Spirit of God. Remember, that by holding these things in, you become a breeding ground to become sick with ulcers, tumors, cancer and other ailments. These illnesses start to manifest if you allow things to fester and overtake you. You have to begin to release those things and give them to God. Ask Him to take care of them for you. God didn't create us for us to be taken out by sickness and disease, He wants to get the glory in your story!

People sometimes tend to hold onto stuff for decades or cover them up and never even deal with them. That is not healthy to do. As mentioned previously, things that are covered up do not heal well. We have to get to the root of the issue and pluck it up from the root.

In our gardens there are many weeds, if we don't pull them from the root, they will continue to sprout up and the process of pulling up the weeds will continue. But if you get the root, there is nothing left to sprout up and you have eliminated the problem at hand. The same is for us and our internal issues, eradicate them at the root.

I've noticed in conversations with others whether they realize or not, that they speak about something like it just happened yesterday. The emotion of anger is still so fresh, which is an indication that it has not yet been dealt with and the root of the situation is still producing unhealthy feelings and shows that the roots have to be destroyed to bring healing and abundance in their life.

Now that I'm older, I realize in past conversations, just a few years back that when I was mentoring and counseling that I had unresolved issues with my father. I would start to tear up when I spoke of certain things pertaining to him. I didn't think the issue was still there, but it was. Even though we are in a good place right now and we're talking and working through some things. I truly believe my transition from adolescent to adulthood would have been easier if I had learned to lean more on my Heavenly Father. Life taught me that man and flesh will fail you every time, but as it is said, "Jesus never fails!"

A Father's hurt is not the child's responsibility!
-Iyanla Vanzant

I truly believe that a lot of fathers don't know how to be fathers. Some had role models and some went through or experienced some kind of short coming or emotional situation in their lives as well. Because of not having stability in their homes as a child, even though they may be trying, they are falling short. Again, we need to look at the possibility of unresolved issues in the man's life that has not been dealt with properly and now it is being passed down to their seed.

So, as we begin to detox and loose some things and truly let it go, we have to make sure that our future generation does not make the same choices or mistakes. Remember we said earlier, "If fatherlessness was a disease, it would be an epidemic." Fatherlessness does take a toll on children, both female and male. It seems to show a greater impact with females, because we are nurturers, givers, producers and givers of life. So, without the role of a father a lot of us would be lost. It's time to accept ownership, be accountable and let go of all that is holding you back.

And I will restore to you the years that the locusts have eaten, the cankerworm, and the caterpillar, and the palmerworm, my great army which I sent among you.
Joel 2:25 KJV

If you're really serious about being healed and delivered, it's time to begin the process to detox all the past hurts, wounds and mistakes from your life. It's time to get focused and get back everything that the enemy stolen from you. All the years of joy stolen from you, get it back and claim it yours. Seek the Lord for direction and get an understanding of what your life should look like, seek Him to know your destiny and your purpose. Release all that weighs you down and walk in the fullness of who He created you to be.

As you go through this detox, you will experience some symptoms. Don't let these things stop you from completing the process. It is important and we need to understand that as you go through this process of letting go, you're going to experience symptoms that will be unpleasant. You may have to surround yourself with people who will support you and also take time to be alone in the presence of God. Sometimes you just need to get quiet and sit still and listen for the voice of God to speak to you and instruct you. The time invested will be valuable and there will be difficult times, but stay with it. You will begin to see the fruits of your labor and you will begin to develop into the person you were created to be, kind of like the cycle of a caterpillar turning into a beautiful butterfly.

You will begin to see yourself differently and see dramatic changes in your life. Things that once bothered you and caused you to be snappy, angry, bitter or those things that would make you raise your voice for no reason, now no longer affect you. You're calmer and more peaceful. What is actually taking place is the inner most parts of you are healing and your spirit is surrendering to God and your spirit is releasing the years of bondage and you are letting it go. No longer holding onto those heavy weights and the end result is you're feeling better and becoming the authentic you, a healthy you, a joyous you; a healed, delivered and set free you! Glory to God!

CHAPTER 12

REDEEMING THE TIME

> *The Spirit of the Lord is upon me, because he has anointed me to preach the gospel to the poor, he has sent me to heal the brokenhearted to preach deliverance to the captives and recovering of sight to the blind, to sit at liberty them that are bruised to preach the acceptable year of the Lord.*
> **Luke 4:18–19 KJV**

I believe every pain has purpose to your promise and know that we all have a testimony to share. You would think it should be easy to break free and not get stuck in stagnant as we go through this thing, we call life. You may think that you wasted years going through turbulent situations and you may feel as though your life has not gone anywhere because issues from your past resurfaces from time to time. Don't be discouraged because there is Good News! God has already planned for every infraction, every detour, every mistake, and every set back that has occurred in your life. He promised to always be there for you and He wants you to know that you are no longer a victim to your situations and issues, but you are victorious over all things. You are free. When you were born, He already knew what you were going to do before you did it.

God's time is like a thousand years to us and one day to Him. He moves in time. We tend to focus on a time schedule that is man-made verses God ordained. We need to learn to move in God's timing and not compare ourselves to others. We want to redeem our time and make sure that we are using time wisely. I'm pretty sure a lot of us have wasted so much time over the years, but know that God can redeem time for us. Just like He can give back time, He also can prolong things. He is in control and can get us caught up to the place He desires us to be, that's the good news.

> *"To everything there is a season, and a time to every purpose under the heaven; a time to be born, a time to die, a time to plant, a time to plug that which is planted; a time to kill, and a time to heal, it's hard to break down, it's hard to build up; a time to weep, and a time to laugh and a time to mourn..."*
> ***Ecclesiastes 3:1-4KJV***

He can give us recompense. What is recompense? Recompense is God's way of giving us something as a way of compensation or a way to make amends to someone for loss or harm suffered. He gives restitution to victims by making them victorious.

Sometimes you may not know how or you may not know when, but regardless of what it looks like, He will provide. It may not come when you want it, but He is always on time. Just remember that delayed does not mean denied, it could be His way of drawing you closer to Him. We have to also remember that the bible tells us in Isaiah 55:8-9 that, "For my thoughts are not your thoughts, neither are your ways my ways, saith the Lord. For as the heavens are higher than the earth, so are my ways higher than your ways, and my thoughts than your thoughts." This means that He gives grace and mercy to us.

    While giving us grace and mercy, He also figuratively turns back the hands of time and restores the things we lost back to us or even gives us better than we had previously. He wants us to now use time wisely because He has given us yet another chance. He doesn't just give second changes because if that were they case, all of us would have messed that opportunity up already too, but He is the God of another chance and sometimes we have to do things a second, third, fourth, fifth… time before we really comprehend and understand what it is that we are doing wrong or incorrectly. He gives us so many chances, but that is because of His grace and mercy given to us.

Despite the fact He has extended to us grace and mercy, it is also up to us to work what He's given us to do. He gives us ample opportunities to get it right with Him and Him only. So, no more revisiting the past, no more doing drive-bys and no more recalling memories of old. We are now thanking Him for the new thing and we're putting away the old thing to make room for the new. We are now new creatures in Christ and trading our ashes for beauty.

I guess you're wondering, "How can I truly make a transition from being fatherless to a daddy's girl?" Well, in order for us to move on and to be healed and forgiven, we truly have to reach out to our Heavenly Father. This has to be first priority before we can do anything else. Why do you ask? Because our Heavenly Father will give you the strength, desire and power within to release and surrender all. You can surrender that built up anger, the bitterness, and resentment that has been carried for years and possibly decades. You absolutely cannot do this in your own strength. Don't be fooled thinking you can. All these things are wrapped up in your mind, body, emotions and spirit, so you will truly need His strength to overcome and release these things. You need Him because your flesh won't let you do it and it's only through coming to the Heavenly Father that you can be healed, delivered and set free from the captives holding your members (mind, will, body, emotions, etc.) in bondage.

Seeking assistance from a counselor is also a wise thing to do if you know you need help. There seems to be a stigma when it comes to asking for help and receiving the assistance needed to overcome tragedies in one's life. Mental health is a serious problem, so please, don't fall into any traps that makes you feel less than a person if you seek the assistance of a counselor. The services are there for you, God created counselors, so use their service.

"Get all the advice and instruction you can, so you will be wise the rest of your life."
Proverbs 19:20 NLT

Of course, I understand everyone that reads this book may not have a spiritual relationship with the Heavenly Father. It is my prayer that by the end of this book that everyone can come into the knowledge of our Lord Jesus Christ and receive the salvation that is waiting for them. Also, I understand that everyone may not have a broken relationship with their biological father, I know there are some that may have never met their biological father or they may have someone who is a father figure but the relationship is not stable or fulfilling. The family unit is so complex in some situations, but we know that whether girl or boy, male or female that we all have a certain connection that lingers with a father figure. God made it so that we have two parents, so I believe that it is His intension for both parents to be present in one's life. So just because our stories may vary, just know that we are all linked by the Heavenly Father.

Thank God for second chances, thank God for He is the redeemer of time, He is the God of recompense. As you surrender to Him and begin to develop a relationship with Him and know Him on a higher level, it won't take long before you will begin to see just how much He loves you.

I know that in my testimony, my relationship with the Heavenly Father is what kept me sane and it kept me in my right mind, He actually kept me from committing suicide. This is why it is so important to know the Heavenly Father as our personal savior.

The love from Abba Father cannot compare to a biological father. You may have been fatherless, but you can still be Daddy's girl. The Heavenly Father promised in His word that He would never leave us nor for sake us. He showers us with Agape love, which is defined as unconditional love. There is nothing, absolutely nothing on earth that we can do to turn the Father's love toward us away. His love is without condition and never ending. Just know that when you are in a relationship with the Heavenly Father, you are Daddy's girl. You are the apple of His eye and He is always looking out for you. He even sent His Precious Holy Spirit to come dwell within you to be your guild as you go through life.

Oftentimes we want to think of our earthly fathers as heroes, but sometimes they aren't always there. It's not fair to compare the Heavenly Father to our earthly father because our earthly father is flesh, he is human. Flesh and spirit do not mix. The flesh is always at war with the spirit and they don't mix well, it's almost like oil and water. No matter how much you shake them together eventually they separate, that is how the flesh interacts with the spirit. In order to be able to operate in the Spirit, the flesh must decrease and submit to the spirit, but if the earthly father does not have a healthy relationship with the Heavenly Father, there will be a constant battle at hand, which may cause him to have an improper relationship with his children.

Through transitioning, I had to do several things, I had to pray to my Heavenly Father to forgive me for my sins. I asked Him to regulate my thought process so that it would align with His ways. I had to ask for the ability to forgive myself for holding onto all of those issues. I knew I had to let them go so they would no longer haunt my life and so they wouldn't continue to manifest in my adulthood.

My next step was to make amends with my father. To make amends is more than an apology, it is defined to compensate or make up for a wrongdoing. It was a vital part for my personal growth and key to me obtaining the healing I needed. The healing I was seeking was not only for me but also for others who I had inadvertently hurt while I was hurting. It is said that hurt people, hurt people. That's what

I did. By making amends with my father, it has allowed us to have yet another chance to reconnect and develop a relationship. When I reached out to my earthly father, I had to come to terms with my role in the equation. I had to say, in spite of all that happened and all the pain I felt regarding you not being in my life the way I wanted you to be, I still love you and I forgive you. I may not understand everything still and probably never will, but having you in my life now is more important than continuing life without you and separated by these questions of Why. I desire to build from where we are now.

When I say God is a God of recompense, He gives you back double and He will restore all the years that the palmerworm and the cankerworm have eaten up. He can give you time back in that person and make those days more precious and valuable than ever. Just know all things are done in God's timing and remember that despite relationship with your earthly father, you are always Daddy's girl with your Heavenly Father.

I hope and pray that my testimony has been a blessing to all have read. I pray you have been truly blessed in your search for the true love which is always given by your Heavenly Father. Smile, you're Daddy's Girl!

REFERENCES

- Bible Translations – King James Version, New Living Translation, Amplified and New International Version
- Sources: US. Census Bureau, America's Families and Living Arrangements: 2011. Characteristics, March 2011 Washington DC; Tables C8
- Source: Osbourne, Cynthia and McLanahans, Sara – Partnership Instability and Child Well-Being, October 2007.
- Quotes from Father's.com inspirational.
- Quote from Steve Harvey – 2013
- Quotes from Dr. Michelle Watson – License Professional Counselor.
- Quotes from Iyanla Vanzant – License Professional Counselor.

- John Eckhardt's, Prayers That Rout Demons', prayers for defeating demons overthrowing the powers of darkness, September 24, 2010.
- Charts and Graphs

www.ingramcontent.com/pod-product-compliance
Lightning Source LLC
Chambersburg PA
CBHW032130090426
42743CB00007B/535